The Star in
the Pail

The Star in the Pail

by David McCord

Illustrated by Marc Simont

Little, Brown and Company

BOSTON   TORONTO

Poems for the Young
by David McCord

FAR AND FEW	PEN, PAPER, AND POEM
TAKE SKY	MR. BIDERY'S SPIDERY GARDEN*
ALL DAY LONG	AWAY AND AGO
EVERY TIME I CLIMB A TREE	THE STAR IN THE PAIL
Illustrated by Marc Simont	*Illustrated by Marc Simont*
FOR ME TO SAY	*Published in England only

TEXT COPYRIGHT © 1925, 1929, 1931, 1941, 1949, 1952, 1960, 1961, 1962, 1965, 1968, 1971, 1972, 1973, 1974, 1975 BY DAVID MCCORD

ILLUSTRATIONS COPYRIGHT © 1975 BY MARC SIMONT

FIRST EDITION

T 11/75

"Hitchhiker" was published in the *Boston Globe.*

"Secret" appeared in *Cricket*; "Christmas Eve" in the Boston *Herald*; "From the kitchen" in *Yankee.*

"How to Draw a Monkey" reprinted by permission from the January 1969 issue of *Good Housekeeping* magazine, © 1969 by the Hearst Corporation.

"Gone" is reprinted by permission of Holt, Rinehart and Winston, Inc., from *Pen, Paper and Poem* by David McCord. © 1973 by Holt, Rinehart and Winston, Inc.

Library of Congress Cataloging in Publication Data

McCord, David Thompson Watson, 1897–
    The star in the pail.

    SUMMARY: Twenty-nine poems involving such diversified topics as starfish, spring, loose teeth, animal crackers, and secrets.
    [1. American poetry] I. Simont, Marc. II. Title.
PZ8.3.M133St   811'.5'2   75-15605
ISBN 0-316-55515-0

Published simultaneously in Canada
by Little, Brown & Company (Canada) Limited

PRINTED IN THE UNITED STATES OF AMERICA

CONTENTS

1 THE STAR IN THE PAIL

I took the pail for water when the sun was high
And left it in the shadow of the barn nearby.

When evening slippered over like the moth's brown wing,
I went to fetch the water from the cool wellspring.

The night was clear and warm and wide, and I alone
Was walking by the light of stars as thickly sown

As wheat across the prairie, or the first fall flakes,
Or spray upon the lawn—the kind the sprinkler makes.

But every star was far away as far can be,
With all the starry silence sliding over me.

And every time I stopped I set the pail down slow,
For when I stooped to pick the handle up to go

Of all the stars in heaven there was one to spare,
And he silvered in the water and I left him there.

2 CHANT

The cow has a cud
The turtle has mud
The rabbit has a hutch
But I haven't much

The ox has a yoke
The frog has a croak
The toad has a wart
So he's not my sort

The mouse has a hole
The polecat a pole
The goose has a hiss
And it goes like this

The duck has a pond
The bird has beyond
The hen has a chick
But I feel sick

The pig has a pen
The bear has a den
The trout has a pool
While I have school

The crow has a nest
The hawk has a quest
The owl has a mate
Doggone! I'm late!

3 ALL ABOUT FIREFLIES
ALL ABOUT

The stars are all so far away
For creature-kind that hide by day—
For moth and mouse and toad and such—
The starlight doesn't count for much.
And that is why a field at night
In May or June is plaintive, bright
With little lanterns sailing by,
Like stars across a mimic sky,
Just high enough—but not too high.

4 OUR MR. TOAD

Our Mr. Toad
Has a nice abode
Under the first front step.
When it rains he's cool
In a secret pool
Where the water goes
    drip
    drop
    drep.

Our Mr. Toad
Will avoid the road:
He's a private-cellar man.
And it's not much fun
In the broiling sun
When you *have* a good
    ten
    tone
    tan.

Our Mr. Toad
Has a kind of code
That tells him the coast is clear.
Then away he'll hop
With a stop, stop, stop
When the dusk draws
    nigh
    no
    near.

5 LITTLE

Little wind, little sun,
Little tree—only one.
Little bird, little wing,
Little song he can sing.
Little need he should stay,
Little *up*-now, away
Little speck, and he's far
Where all little things are.
Little things for me too:
Little sad that he flew.

6 THE STARFISH

When I see a starfish
Upon the shining sand,
I ask him how he liked the sea
And if he likes the land.
"Would you rather be a starfish
Or an out-beyond-the-bar fish?"
I whisper very softly,
And he seems to understand.

He never *says* directly,
But I fancy all the same
That he knows the answer quite as well
As if it were his name:
"An out-beyond-the-bar fish
Is much happier than a starfish";
And when I look for him again
He's gone the way he came.

7 IN THE MIDDLE

I think about the elephant and flea,
For somewhere in between them there is me.

Perhaps the flea is unaware of this:
Perhaps I'm not what elephants would miss.

I don't know how the flea puts in his day;
I guess an elephant just likes to sway.

But there they are: one little and one large,
And in between them only me in charge!

8 THREE SIGNS OF SPRING

Kite on the end of the twine,
Fish on the end of a line,
Dog on the end of a whine.

Dog on the leash is straining,
Fish on the line is gaining:
Only these two complaining.

Kite is all up in the air,
Kite doesn't quite compare,
Kite doesn't *really* care.

Kite, of course, is controllable;
Dog, with a word, consolable;
Fish hopes he isn't poleable.

Trust the dog for an urge,
Trust the kite for a surge,
Trust the trout to submerge.

Kite in the wind and the rain,
Dog in the woods again,
Fish in his deep domain.

9 TWO TRIOLETS

The birds in the feeder
are fighting again.
Not squirrels in the cedar,
but birds in the feeder.
They haven't a leader:
just eight, nine, or ten
of the birds in the feeder
are fighting again.

It's a foggy day
When winter thaws
And the snow is grey.
It's a foggy day:
O Doggy, go 'way
With your dirty paws!
It's a foggy day
When winter thaws.

10 TOOTH TROUBLE

When I see the dentist
I take him all my teeth:
Some of me's above them,
But most of me's beneath.

And one is in my pocket,
Because it grew so loose
That I could fit a string to it
And tighten up the noose.

I'll grow another, dentist says,
And shall not need to noose it.
Another still to drill and fill?
Not me! I won't produce it.

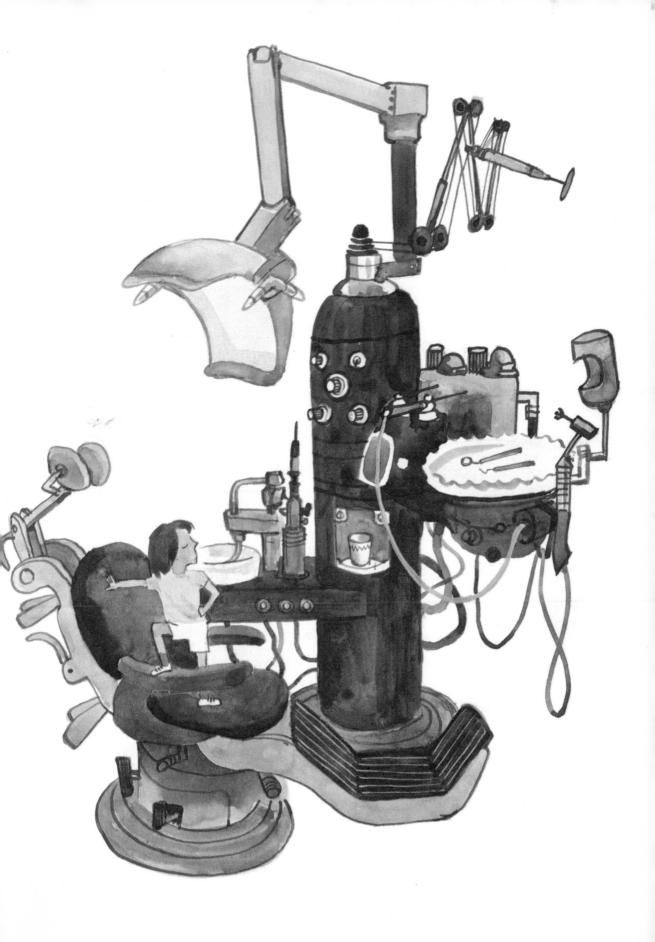

11 THREE LIMERICKS

A man who was fond of his skunk
Thought he smelled pure and pungent as punk.
    But his friends cried No, no,
      No, no, no, no, no, *no!*
He just stinks, or he stank, or he stunk.

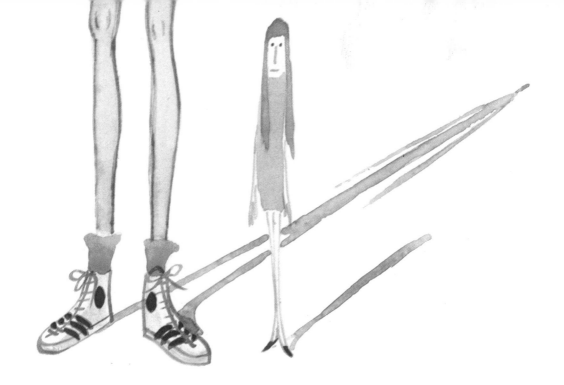

Take the curious case of Tom Pettigrew
And Hetty, his sister. When Hettigrew
 As tall as a tree
 She came just to Tom's knee.
And did *Tom* keep on growing? You bettigrew.

It's been a bad year for the moles
Who live just in stockings with holes;
 And bad for the mice
 Who prefer their boiled rice
Served in shoes that don't have any soles.

12 TICK-TOCK TALK

Big clocks go *tick,*
Big clocks go *tock.*
The ticking always seems to mock

The tocking. Don't the tocks sound thick
Compared with ticks, whose tongues are quick?

"The clock is *ticking,*" people say.
No clocks are ever *tocking.* They

Make just as many tocks as ticks!
It's sad to see tocks in a fix

Like this: I'd love to know some clocks
That have no ticks at all—just tocks.

One thing you'll notice, though, is when
Clocks strike the hour—five or ten,

Or two or six, say; twelve or three—
They're telling you what they tell me

About the tick-tocks: something's *wrong,*
The sour way that clocks go *Bong!*

13 YELLOW

Green is go,
and red is stop,
and yellow is peaches
with cream on top.

Earth is brown,
and blue is sky;
yellow looks well
on a butterfly.

Clouds are white,
black, pink, or mocha;
yellow's a dish of
tapioca.

14 CHRISTMAS EVE

My stocking's where
He'll see it—there!
One-half a pair.

The tree is sprayed,
My prayers are prayed,
My wants are weighed.

I've made a list
Of what he missed
Last year. I've kissed

My father, mother,
Sister, brother;
I've done those other

Things I should
And would and could.
So far, so good.

15 HITCHHIKER

There was a witch who met an owl.
He flew beside her, wing to jowl.

Owl language always pleased the witch:
Her owl at home sat in his niche
And talked a lot about the bats
He met at night, and how the cats
Were scared of him. That sort of thing.
But here was one owl on the wing,
Who said—I don't mean said "Who, who!"—
Who said, "I've just escaped the zoo.
I'm going home. I haven't flown
Much lately—that is, on my own.
They flew me to the zoo, you know,
Last . . . well, it's several years ago.

"My wings are stiff: I'm tired! *Am* I!
So when I saw you flying by,
I thought 'She's heading north by east.
If I can hitch a ride at least
As far as Pocono, I'll make
It home.' Okay? Is that a rake
Or broom you're flying? Sure! A broom.

"I see it is. Nice model. Room
Enough along the handle for
An owl to perch. Thanks! You can pour
It on! A little shut-eye's what
I need."

      I guess that's what he got.

16 FROM THE KITCHEN

PISTACHIO ICE CREAM

Pistachio ice cream, all green;
And I am pausing now between
Two spoonfuls just to say I wish
You had the money for a dish.

ANIMAL CRACKERS

Animal crackers! I ate them years
Before you did. It now appears
That Indian crackers and cowboy cousins
Are eaten by the million dozens.
These new ones may look good to you,
But I am useter to the zoo.

PEOPLE CRACKERS

People crackers! Or don't you know
They make them now for dogs, just so
That poor old Rover can enjoy
A little girl, a little boy,
While you are munching if you please
On lions, tigers, chimpanzees;
On hippos, zebras, tall giraffes;
On mean hyenas full of laughs.

17 THE SHELL

I took away the ocean once,
Spiraled in a shell,
And happily for months and months
I heard it very well.

How is it then that I should hear
What months and months before
Had blown upon me sad and clear,
Down by the grainy shore?

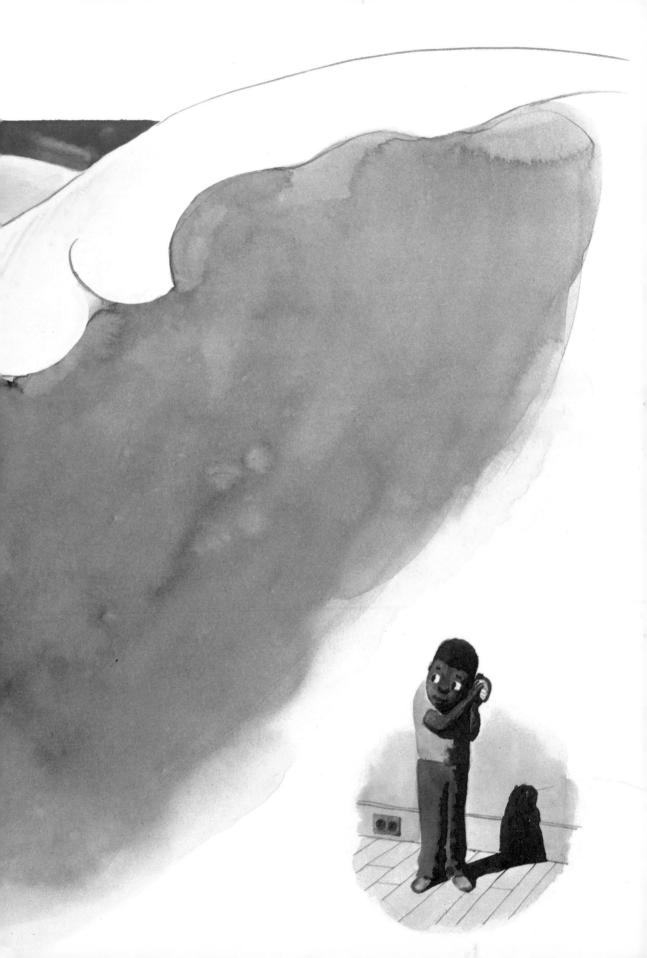

18 MR. MIXUP TELLS A STORY

Under the rabbit there, I saw a tree—
Well, you know what I mean.
His ears were green and leafy . . . you asked me
to *tell* you, didn't you, just what I'd seen?

Well, anyhow, out peered that big red box.
Red fox? Did I say *box?* A fox it was!
He didn't see me. I looked up my clocks . . .
My *watch?* My watch to watch how long he does.

How long he *took?* A nice word, *took.* That's right . . .
to spot my rabbit up above his spine—
his pine. No, rabbits don't have wings. It's quite
enough to wiggle nose. Can't wiggle mine.

Ten days went by. You say *ten minutes?* Why?
Because it happened yesterday? It should.
Then suddenly I saw the fellow fly.
Which fellow? Couldn't he? Oh, yes, he could.

And that old boxed-up wolf. I tell you he . . .
I don't know which direction. What's the diff?
He didn't catch—he wasn't after *me.*
What rabbit? Well, speak up! No matter if.

19 SNOWFLAKES

Sometime this winter if you go
To walk in soft new-falling snow
When flakes are big and come down slow

To settle on your sleeve as bright
As stars that couldn't wait for night,
You won't know what you have in sight—

Another world—unless you bring
A magnifying glass. This thing
We call a snowflake is the king

Of crystals. Do you like surprise?
Examine him three times his size:
At first you won't believe your eyes.

Stars look alike, but flakes do not:
No two the same in all the lot
That you will get in any spot

You chance to be, for every one
Come spinning through the sky has none
But his own window-wings of sun:

Joints, points, and crosses. What could make
Such lacework with no crack or break?
In billion billions, no mistake?

20 HAMMOCK

Our hammock swings between two trees,
So when the garden's full of bees,
And if the hammock's full of me,
They fly right over, bee by bee.
They fly goshawful fast and straight—
I guess a bee is never late;
And if I can't quite see the line,
I try to think I hear the whine:
Much higher than the drowsy sound
Of having hives of bees around.
Provided bees don't bother me,
I'm glad to let a bee just be.
Some day I'll put a microphone
Inside their door and pipe the drone
Above my hammock, fall asleep
To bees all busy-buzz that keep
Their distance. Meanwhile here I lie.
I'm watching now a butterfly,
Unhurried, knowing not what's up:
A daisy, rose, or buttercup?
Not caring where he's been, or where
He's flapping to. He fills the air
With little flags and floats away
As I do on this summer's day.

21 SECRET

Jean said, *No.*
But Ruth said, *Yes!*
What? said Judy.
Gwyn said, *Guess!*
Where? said Karen.
There! said Claire.
But Lori's eyes said,
I don't care.

HOW TO DRAW A MONKEY

To draw a monkey, don't begin
With him, but what he's on or in.
He's in a tree, he's on a limb,
Or was on one. Just follow him
Or follow me—it's all the same,
But easier with me: I'm tame.
You see the branch he's hanging from?
Don't draw it all, though. Just draw some
Of it—about two inches, say.
And draw it so it doesn't sway.
Next twist ten monkey fingers round
It, way up there above the ground,
And hang two arms from them, straight down.
(If you use color, make it brown.
And if the monkey has to scratch,
You'll have to change my method, natch!)
Now join those arms to shoulders, wide
Apart to keep the head inside.
If you can't make a monkey's face,
Look in the mirror! Then you place
The body underneath the head,
But full of life—he isn't dead;
He's just a monkey hanging there
Without his legs. But oh, beware
Of leaving him, forgetting legs!
Remember, chickens come from eggs,
But monkeys, unlike eggs, don't run:
Without two legs it isn't done.
Be sure that to each leg you add
One foot. And if your drawing pad
Is not quite long enough for toes,
Who cares? The monkey, I suppose.

23 FAST AND SLOW

The Snail is slow. The swift Gazelle
Could never manage with a shell.

The Snail, without his shell, would squirm
And look a lot like half a worm.

To find him, you would need to peek
Inside some nasty robin's beak.

The poor Gazelle must run to stay
Alive. And that's about the way

It is with Snails and swift Gazelles:
Some have, and some do not have, shells.

24 HARVESTMAN

Old Daddy Longlegs, Harvestman,
travels with no particular plan
in mind, so far as I can see:
I meet him wherever he happens to be.
In summer he happens most of all
to be on the sunniest pineboard wall
of a house by a lake. So I say "Hello!
That's a splintery board for stubbing a toe."
He doesn't have toes, of course, but what
do you say to a creature that looks a lot
like a tiny bright pebble with hand-me-down legs,
not a bit good for much except walking on eggs?

25　GONE

I've looked behind the shed
And under every bed:
I think he must be dead.

What reason for alarm?
He doesn't know the farm.
I *knew* he'd come to harm!

He was a city one
Who never had begun
To think the city fun.

Now where could he have got?
He doesn't know a lot.
I haven't heard a shot.

That old abandoned well,
I thought. Perhaps he fell?
He didn't. I could tell.

Perhaps he found a scent:
A rabbit. Off he went.
He'll come back home all spent.

Groundhogs, they say, can fight;
And raccoons will at night.
He'd not know one by sight!

I've called and called his name.
I'll never be the same.
I blame myself . . . I blame . . .

All *he* knows is the park;
And now it's growing dark.
A bark? You *hear* a bark?

26 RUNOVER RHYME

Down by the pool still fishing,
Wishing for fish, I fail;
Praying for birds not present,
Pheasant or grouse or quail.

Up in the woods, his hammer
Stammering, I can't see
The woodpecker, find the cunning
Sunning old owl in tree.

Over the field such raucous
Talk as the crows talk on!
Nothing around me slumbers;
Numbers of birds have gone.

Even the leaves hang listless,
Lasting through days we lose,
Empty of what is wanted,
Haunted by what we choose.